EDGE
BOOKS™

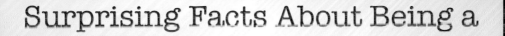
Surprising Facts About Being a

NAVY SAILOR

by Kristin J. Russo

Consultant:
Kurt Waeschle, Chief of Operations
Navy Region Northwest Fire and Emergency Services

Edge Books are published by Capstone Press,
1710 Roe Crest Drive, North Mankato, Minnesota 56003
www.mycapstone.com

Library of Congress Cataloging-in-Publication Data
Names: Russo, Kristin J., author.
Title: Surprising facts about being a Navy sailor / by Kristin J Russo.
Description: North Mankato, Minnesota : Capstone Press, [2018] | Series: Edge
      books. What you didn't know about the U.S. military life | Includes
      bibliographical references and index. | Audience: Grades 4-6. | Audience: Ages 8-14.
Identifiers: LCCN 2017009187| ISBN 9781515774303 (library binding) | ISBN 9781515774341 (ebook pdf)
Subjects: LCSH: United States. Navy--Military life--Juvenile literature.
      Sailors--United States--Juvenile literature.
Classification: LCC VA58.4 .R87 2018 | DDC 359.10973--dc23
LC record available at https://lccn.loc.gov/2017009187

Editorial Credits
Nikki Ramsay, editor; Sara Radka, designer; Laura Manthe, production specialist

Photo Credits
Getty Images: Chip Somodevilla, 9, Chris Hondros, 7, Cody R. Babin/U.S. Navy, 17, Justin Sullivan, 16, Lt. Steve
Smith/U.S. Navy, 15, Patrick Smith, 8, 11, Sandy Huffaker/Stringer, 20; Newscom: Polaris, 27, U.S. Navy/Sipa
USA, cover, 4, 21, 23, ZUMAPRESS/Gary Kieffer, 13, ZUMAPRESS/Mcss Kenneth G. Takada/Planet Pix, 18;
Shutterstock: Boykov, 25, Glynnis Jones, 29, Joseph Sohm, 26, 28, Robert Kneschke, 6; Wikimedia: U.S. Navy/
Photographer's Mate 2nd Class Dawn C. Morrison, 24

Graphic elements by Book Buddy Media.

Printed in the United States of America.
010364F17

TABLE OF CONTENTS

LIFE AT SEA

In ancient times, sailors rammed their warships into enemy boats to try to sink them. They boarded enemy ships using hooks and ramps. After gunpowder was invented, sailors launched cannonballs at enemy ships. They would also set them on fire. Sometimes they destroyed their own ships by mistake.

Today, United States Navy warships can launch **missiles** and **torpedoes** from miles away. Sailors on aircraft carriers still use hooks, but not to capture enemy ships. Hooks and cables are used to stop flying jets so that they can land on deck.

You might know that the Navy has specially trained sailors called SEALs. But did you know that some Navy sailors, called cyber warriors, work to stop attacks on the Internet? And did you know that others are musicians? Some even train dogs to jump out of airplanes. Get ready to learn amazing facts that will open your eyes to what it's really like to be a Navy sailor.

missile—an object that is thrown, shot, or launched as a weapon

torpedo—a bomb that is meant to be fired underwater

Chapter 1

LET'S GO NAVY!

Joining the Navy is not easy. People who want to **enlist** should meet with a **recruiter** first. Recruiters share information and give advice. They also tell people where to go to take the next steps to enlist. These include tests and physical fitness screenings.

The ASVAB Test

Can you do puzzles with oddly shaped puzzle pieces? Do you know why water is heavier than air? These are some of the tests and questions on the Armed Services Vocational Battery (ASVAB) test. Everyone who wants to join the Navy must take the ASVAB. Topics include science, math, reading, electronics, and mechanics. People study very hard for this test. Their scores decide what job they will have and how much they will get paid when they join.

enlist—to voluntarily join a branch of the military

recruiter—a military member who provides guidance to people interested in the armed forces

A career fair is a good place to learn about different types of jobs. U.S. Navy recruiters can answer questions about how to enlist in the Navy.

Requirements and Restrictions

Not everyone is allowed to enlist. People must earn a certain score on the ASVAB and they must have a high school education. Sometimes medical problems can keep people from being allowed to join. Some people are born with extra fingers. Others may have a head or ear injury. People with conditions like these might not be allowed to join. They may not be able to wear standard equipment such as gloves and helmets.

ENROLLING IN THE USNA

Every year, about 17,000 students apply to the U.S. Naval Academy in Annapolis, Maryland. Only about 1,300 are accepted. First-year students are called plebes. Students in their second through fourth years are called midshipmen.

Plebes push through grueling tests to become physically and mentally stronger.

Plebe Summer

Before the school year officially begins, students attend a summer training session. It is called "Plebe Summer." Students may not watch television or use their cell phones. They must get special permission to call home. They exercise hard every day in the summer heat. Between 10 and 20 people drop out before school starts.

Midshipmen

After they have attended a full year at the academy, students become midshipmen. Midshipmen exercise together early in the morning. They do marching drills at night. During the summer, they do not go home for vacation like most college students. Midshipmen are assigned to serve on Navy ships or submarines. When midshipmen graduate, they automatically become officers called **ensigns**.

 **FACT** When plebes complete their first year, they do the "Herndon Climb." First, a monument for Commander William Lewis Herndon (1813-1857) is covered with grease. Then, the entire plebe class works together to remove a Dixie cup hat that is placed at the top. Legend has it that the plebe who grabs the cup will be the first **admiral** from the class.

ensign—an officer of the lowest rank in the U.S. Navy

admiral—the highest type of ranking officer in the U.S. Navy

Chapter 2

FULL SPEED AHEAD

BASIC TRAINING

From the minute they set foot in boot camp, Navy sailors are always training — for the next job, rank, or mission. There is always something new to learn.

Fitness Test

When they first arrive at basic training, recruits take a physical fitness test. About 50 percent of them fail the test the first time. After exercising six days per week for eight weeks, most recruits pass the test. Only 5 to 10 percent fail the physical fitness test at the end of boot camp.

"The Unluckiest Ship in the Navy"

Recruits are trained on the USS *Trayer*, which is jokingly called "the unluckiest ship in the Navy." That's because everything on the USS *Trayer* is supposed to go wrong.

The ship was made by Hollywood movie set designers to simulate the actual sights, sounds, and smells of a real ship. Recruits learn how to put out engine fires and respond to real emergencies that they might face at sea. They face pretend missile attacks, and learn how to cope with simulated deaths, injuries, and damage to the ship.

While events that happen on the USS *Trayer* are not real, recruits still feel the pressure. They must pass the USS *Trayer* simulation test in order to complete boot camp.

Recruits at boot camp work, live, and train as a team. They learn to help one another complete challenging tasks.

Being "Recycled"

The Navy has nearly 43,000 recruits per year. Every one of them attends boot camp at the Naval Station Great Lakes near Lake Michigan in Illinois.

There are many important rules that recruits must follow. They must salute everyone who outranks them. They must iron their uniforms perfectly. They are required to make their beds, or "racks," by folding perfect 45-degree angles at the corners.

Recruits who make mistakes face penalties such as being "recycled." Being recycled means a sailor is sent back to an earlier segment of boot camp and must do difficult drills all over again. A recycled sailor might be sent out in the cold to shovel snow early in the morning. Recruits at boot camp try not to make any mistakes to avoid these kinds of penalties.

SEAL TRAINING

Sailors who want to join the Navy's special forces team, called SEALs, must complete a harsh training program called Basic Underwater Demolition/SEAL (BUD/S) training.

Hell Week

About 70 percent of sailors who enter BUD/S training drop out. Only 25 percent make it through the first phase. This phase includes a segment called "Hell Week." For five days in a row, trainees never stop exercising. They swim for miles in the ocean, run in the sand, and march carrying heavy logs. During this five-day period, they sleep for a total of only four hours.

Training Misery

SEAL trainees are cold, wet, sore, and tired most of the time. Some trainees pass out during drills. Although it is very rare, some have even drowned. Trainees must drop out if they are injured.

Giving Up

In order to quit, trainees must ring a bronze bell. Ringing the bell is a public way of saying, "I give up." Many trainees push through the misery because they feel that ringing the bell would be worse.

FACT Christopher Kyle (1974–2013) wrote an autobiography about his experiences on four deployments to Iraq as a Navy SEAL. His story was made into a major Hollywood movie called *American Sniper*. Kyle was played by actor Bradley Cooper in the film.

During Hell Week, trainees face many challenges. Sitting in the cold ocean water is a test of endurance and mental strength.

Chapter 3

ON DECK

A CITY AT SEA

Living on an aircraft carrier is like living on a "city at sea." Aircraft carriers are the largest of all types of Navy ships. They have their own post offices, hospitals, barbershops, chapels, and even their own zip codes! Life on board an aircraft carrier also comes with its own unique problems.

Dangers on Deck

One of the main jobs of an aircraft carrier is to be a landing site for airplanes. Because of this, an aircraft carrier's deck is a huge, noisy, and dangerous place. As a jet flies in to land, sailors arrange cables that are snagged by a hook on the plane's tail. Once one jet has landed, sailors quickly reset the cables to prepare for another landing. Aircraft landings sometimes take place only seconds apart.

There is always a risk that an accident might happen in a place where hundreds of people work with airplanes. In 1991, Petty Officer J.D. Bridges was a sailor on an aircraft carrier when he got sucked into a jet's **intake**. Luckily the pilots quickly turned off the engine and Bridges survived his close call with the engine's spinning blades.

FACT Aircraft carriers are about 3 football fields long and can have more than 18 deck levels. It takes 5,000 to 6,000 sailors to operate one.

Aircraft of all kinds take off and land on the USS *John C. Stennis*. The aircraft carrier can travel 1 million miles (1,609,344 kilometers) before it needs to refuel.

Dangers Below Deck

Sailors who work below deck also face dangers posed by fire and explosions. In May 1990, a fire broke out in the boiler room of a Navy destroyer. One sailor was killed and 12 suffered burns and other injuries.

In 2015, the Navy introduced a possible solution to dangerous fires on board Navy ships. A robot named SAFFiR (Shipboard Autonomous Firefighting Robot) is being developed to help detect and fight fires in tight spaces below deck.

The robot is about the size of an average man at 5 feet, 10 inches (180 centimeters) tall and about 140 pounds (64 kilograms). It has special sensors and cameras that allow it to see through smoke to find heat sources. It can even hold a fire hose to put the fire out.

intake—a place or part where liquid or air enters something

15

When sailors "man the rails," they stand along the rails of the ship when it enters a port or returns to its home port after a deployment.

Gaining Your Sea Legs

No one knows why motion sickness happens or how to stop it. About 70 percent of people feel dizzy and sick to their stomachs when they are out at sea. These people are likely suffering from motion sickness.

Navy researchers have studied motion sickness by spinning people around in a movable chair. However, the rolling ocean does not act like a spinning chair. Sailors cannot stop the ocean from constantly moving. Some medications can help, but they can also make people tired. Navy sailors have to overcome motion sickness simply by getting used to it. For sailors, this is called "gaining your sea legs."

Surgery at Sea

Illnesses and injuries on a Navy ship can be much more serious than seasickness. The USS *America*, the Navy's newest aircraft carrier, has a hospital on board. Doctors provide medical care to anyone who becomes ill or has an accident.

The USS *America*'s hospital has two operating rooms, a three-bed intensive care unit, and a 23-bed recovery area. Surgeries are not performed if the water is too choppy.

When their fishing boat broke down, five Filipino fishermen drifted for three days without food in the Philippine Sea. They received help from medical personnel aboard the USS *Blue Ridge* after they were rescued in March 2015.

LIFE ON A SUBMARINE

Submarines are tiny compared to aircraft carriers, yet they are still large enough to carry more than 100 people. The crew breathes air that is created by passing electricity through seawater. In a process called electrolysis, the hydrogen and oxygen molecules that make up the water are separated. The oxygen is stored in pressurized canisters for submariners to breathe. There is always enough air on a nuclear submarine, no matter how long it stays underwater.

The USS *Maine* usually has 15 officers and 140 enlisted sailors on board.

Taking Out the Trash

A submarine does not need to surface for air or for supplies while on a mission. All supplies are packed on board. So where does the trash go? Sailors melt and flatten garbage, and throw it away when they return to port. Food waste is released into the ocean for the fish to eat.

To Dive and Rise

Submarines have tanks that can be filled with either water or air. When the crew wants the submarine to submerge, they discharge the air in their tanks and fill the tanks with water. This causes the submarine to drop below the surface. To return to the surface, they use compressed air that pushes them back to the top.

Escape

Most submariners work and live in the inner hull, which is called the "people tank." It is everyone's job to make sure no water leaks into the people tank. If there is a fire or leak, the crew can escape by sealing themselves into an escape hatch. A rescue vehicle that can go as deep as 2,000 feet (610 meters) will rush to their aid.

WORKING ON A SUBMARINE

Working on a submarine is difficult and dangerous. Only a select few are chosen to work on submarines. Submarines do not have windows or portholes. Sailors can only see the surface of the ocean through a **periscope**. All submariners must go through special training. They learn how to drive the ship, do damage control in case of a leak or fire, and use the submarine as a weapon. Submariners who complete this training are said to have "earned their dolphins." Because submarine deployments are mentally and physically difficult, only sailors who have volunteered for an underwater mission are allowed to serve on one.

Staying in Good Spirits

Receiving excellent nutrition is important to doing any job well. Military food is not known for being tasty, but submariners eat tasty, hearty meals — called "five-star grub" — so they always look forward to meal time. They can also exercise on treadmills and stationary bicycles. Submariners work and sleep on the same day-and-night schedule they would follow if they were on land. This has helped sailors stay healthy and alert.

periscope—a device used in a submarine that allows the sailors inside the vessel to see what is happening above the water

Security checks are conducted on submarines to keep crew members safe.

FACT On April 10, 1963, the USS *Thresher* sank below crush depth and all 129 people on the nuclear submarine were lost. As a result, the Navy developed Deep Submergence Rescue Vehicles (DSRV) that can help carry sailors in a sinking submarine to safety. The DSRVs help submariners in the U.S. Navy and in foreign navies.

Chapter 4

WORKING ON LAND AND IN THE AIR

Not all Navy personnel serve at sea. There are hundreds of very important jobs for Navy personnel on land and in the air. Some of these jobs are unusual and their duties might surprise you!

Dog Handlers

Dog handlers usually take care of military dogs in addition to their regular job. Navy dogs work very hard standing guard and sniffing out bombs. They cannot do this alone. They need humans to teach them and guide them. Dog handlers feed, exercise, and train their military dogs every day.

Some military dogs are trained to join the elite Navy SEALs. Most SEAL dogs are Belgian Malinois, a breed similar to German shepherds, but slightly smaller and more compact. SEAL dogs are trained to parachute into combat zones, sometimes in tandem with a human SEAL, and sometimes on their own.

Dogs wear oxygen masks and skin protectors as well as fitted eyewear called "doggles." These special goggles have infrared technology that helps dogs see at night and see heat through buildings. The dogs enter danger zones first, wearing video cameras so that their handlers can see potential trouble, before human SEALs follow.

Dog handlers work with their canines to keep military bases secure. These dogs are very good at detecting and tracking intruders.

Cyber Warriors

The Navy relies on computer technology. If an enemy hacker shuts down communication, steals information, or uploads a virus, the Navy's information networks could be at a serious risk. It is the cyber warrior's job to patrol **cyberspace** and to prevent security **breaches**.

Cyber warriors are computer whizzes. Their job is to protect online networks from hackers and information thieves. The first 27 cyber warriors trained at the USNA graduated in 2016. They are the first line of defense for the Navy against foreign cyberwarfare and **espionage**.

cyberspace—the online world of computer networks and the Internet

breach—an occurrence in which someone is able to get into a place that is guarded, or is able to get secret information

espionage—the activity of spying

THE BLUE ANGELS

The Blue Angels are the U.S. Navy's flight demonstration team. The squadron was created in 1946 to attract new recruits to join the Navy as pilots. Today, there are 17 officers on the team, and six of them fly at once.

Flight Aerobatics

The Blue Angels' planes can fly at almost twice the speed of sound — about 1,400 miles (2,253 km) per hour. However, during public flight demonstrations, they are only allowed to fly up to about 700 miles (1,127 km) per hour. They spin, roll, and dart in and out of formation. In the daring Diamond 360 maneuver, they fly only 18 inches (46 centimeters) apart. Pilots clench their leg and stomach muscles to keep blood from rushing to their head. This keeps them from passing out in midair.

Working Together

The pilots do everything in unison, even when they're not in the air. For example, when the leader of the squadron takes his or her sunglasses off, they all must take their sunglasses off. If the leader wears a jacket, they all must wear the same jacket. This helps the pilots bond so that they fly in better unison in the air.

The Blue Angels fly over big sporting events, such as the Super Bowl, to thrill audiences.

ARTS AND PHOTOGRAPHY

Some sailors become mass communication specialists. They write about and take pictures of important Navy events. They sometimes film underwater combat with a special underwater camera. They may also photograph troops on the battlefield as combat cameramen.

Navy mass communication specialists travel around the world. They record historic military events and produce news articles for newspapers, magazines, television, and radio.

In addition to performing at parades and ceremonies, the U.S. Navy band makes recordings of its music. These recordings are sent for free to libraries, schools, and veterans' organizations that request them.

Mass communication specialists may take unusual photos. For example, some specialists record the condition of underwater vehicles before they are used on deployment.

MUSICIANS

Not all Navy sailors carry weapons. Some carry saxophones, trumpets, flutes, and drums. They are Navy musicians. They are recruited for their musical talents and play in one of many Navy bands. Musicians rarely see combat, but they are still required to complete boot camp and keep themselves in good physical condition.

Musicians must audition for a spot in a Navy band. Most hope to play for the United States Navy Band in Washington, D.C., or the Naval Academy Band in Annapolis, Maryland. Others will play in smaller, regional bands. They march in parades and perform special concerts at the Pentagon and Arlington National Cemetery.

Chapter 5

SPEAKING LIKE A SAILOR

Navy sailors have their own language, and they often use old words that no one hears anymore. This language helps the sailors take orders quickly without confusion.

Aye, Aye

The late 17th to the 18th centuries were considered the Golden Age of Piracy. Mates on a pirate ship would say, "Aye, aye, Captain," in reply to an order. The term "aye, aye" is alive and well on today's Navy ships. All Navy sailors must say this in response to a command. It means they have understood their orders and will carry them out.

Mayday!

Other words are borrowed from other languages. Navy sailors shout "Mayday!" when they are in extreme danger. Nearby boats will rush to help the ship in trouble. It comes from the French word *m'aidez*, which means "help me."

FACT Civilians use "mayday" when they have a boating emergency. Making a false "mayday" call is illegal. The punishment is up to six years in prison and a fine of $250,000.

Sailors often have to work with ropes and "bights." A bight is a loop of rope that is sometimes used to tie a knot.

Port and Starboard

Sailors also swap everyday words for **nautical** terms. Sailors often refer to "left" and "right" as "port" and "starboard," even when they are not on a boat. The word "starboard" comes from the **Old English** word for "steering side." Since most rowers were right-handed, the boat would be steered from the right. The left side always faced "port" to make it easier to load and unload the ship.

nautical—relating to ships and sailing

Old English—the English language before AD 1100

GLOSSARY

admiral (AD-muh-ruhl)—the highest type of ranking officer in the U.S. Navy

breach (BREECH)—an occurrence in which someone is able to get into a place that is guarded, or is able to get secret information.

cyberspace (SY-buhr-SPAYSS)—the online world of computer networks and the Internet

enlist (in-LIST)—to voluntarily join a branch of the military

ensign (in-SIYN)—an officer of the lowest rank in the U.S. Navy

espionage (ESS-pee-uh-nahzh)—the activity of spying

intake (in-TAYK)—a place or part where liquid or air enters something

missile (MISS-uhl)—an object that is thrown, shot, or launched as a weapon

nautical (NAW-tuh-kuhl)—relating to ships and sailing

Old English (OLD IN-glish)—the English language before AD 1100

periscope (PER-uh-skope)—a device used in a submarine that allows the sailors inside the vessel to see what is happening above the water

recruiter (ri-KROOT-uhr)—a military member who provides guidance to people interested in the armed forces

torpedo (tor-PEE-doh)—a bomb that is meant to be fired underwater

READ MORE

Goldish, Meish. *Dolphins in the Navy.* America's Animal Soldiers. New York: Bearport Publishing, 2012.

Gunderson, Jessica. *U.S. Navy True Stories: Tales of Bravery.* Courage Under Fire. Mankato, Minn.: Capstone Press, 2015.

Micklos, John, Jr. *SEAL Team Six: Battling Terrorism Worldwide.* Mankato, Minn.: Capstone Press, 2017.

INTERNET SITES

Use FactHound to find Internet sites related to this book.

Visit *www.facthound.com*

Just type in 9781515774303 and go.

Check out projects, games and lots more at
www.capstonekids.com

INDEX